Published in the UK by
LITTLE **BLACK**DOG LIMITED
Unit 3 Everdon Park
Heartlands Business Park
NN11 8YJ

Telephone   01327 871 777
Facsimile   01327 879 222
E Mail info@littleblackdogltd.co.uk

Copyright © 2008 SILVEY-JEX PARTNERSHIP
Cover and interior layout by Sanjit Saha @ Little Black Dog

ISBN 9781904967675

D1584632

Printed and bound in the UK

LOVE & PASSION FOR THE ELDERLY

BY THE
SILVEY JEX PARTNERSHIP

HELLO HANDSOME!

ARE YOU FOLLOWING ME YOUNG MAN?

SIGH! BY THE TIME WE'VE GOT OUR CLOTHES OFF, THE MOOD WILL HAVE GONE!

YES IT'S VERY NICE MR POTTER... NOW WHAT'S THIS ABOUT AN INGROWING TOE NAIL?

YOU'RE SUPPOSED TO GO TO SLEEP AFTER IT...NOT DURING IT!

YO SWEET SISTERS - EVERYTHING'S COOL. WHICH BABE'S GONNA CHECK OUT WITH SUPER STUD AND GIT ON DOWN TO MY LOVE THANG!

I'VE LEFT MY TEETH SOMEWHERE...
YOU HAVEN'T SEEN THEM HAVE YOU JEFFERY?

I'M TINGLING WITH EXCITEMENT—OR IT COULD BE MY POOR CIRCULATION

IT'S ALRIGHT OLD GIRL...I'M WEARING A CATHETER

IT'S LOVELY HERBERT – JUST WHAT I'VE ALWAYS WANTED

WHY CAN'T YOU SLEEP AFTER LUNCH LIKE <u>OTHER</u> OLD MEN?

...I HOPE YOU'RE READY FOR THIS MY DEAR...
I'VE GOT SOME JUMP LEADS ATTACHED TO THE YOUNG MAN NEXT DOOR

OH MR MARCO YOU SEXY BEAST—
LET'S GO BACK TO MY PLACE AFTER THE SHOW AND MAKE LOVE

TYING ME TO THE BED IS OKAY... BUT DID YOU <u>HAVE</u> TO USE A GRANNY KNOT?

FUNNY... WHEN I WAS YOUNG I ALWAYS FANCIED AN OLDER MAN... BUT NOW...

NO, NO - I SAID...I'VE GOT ACUTE <u>ANGINA</u> !!

AFTER YOU WITH THE TEETH, MY DARLING

STAY DOWN THERE MISS WILKINS, I THINK I HEAR MATRON COMING

...AND LOOK AT THE SHODDY CRAFTSMANSHIP ON THESE...
THEY'VE FORGOTTEN TO STITCH THE CROTCH UP.

DON'T LOOK DEAR.... THEY'LL ONLY GET SILLY

IF YOU'RE FREE...I'M FREE AND I MEAN <u>FREE</u>

I'D BETTER NOT GO DOWN.... I WON'T BE ABLE TO GET UP AGAIN

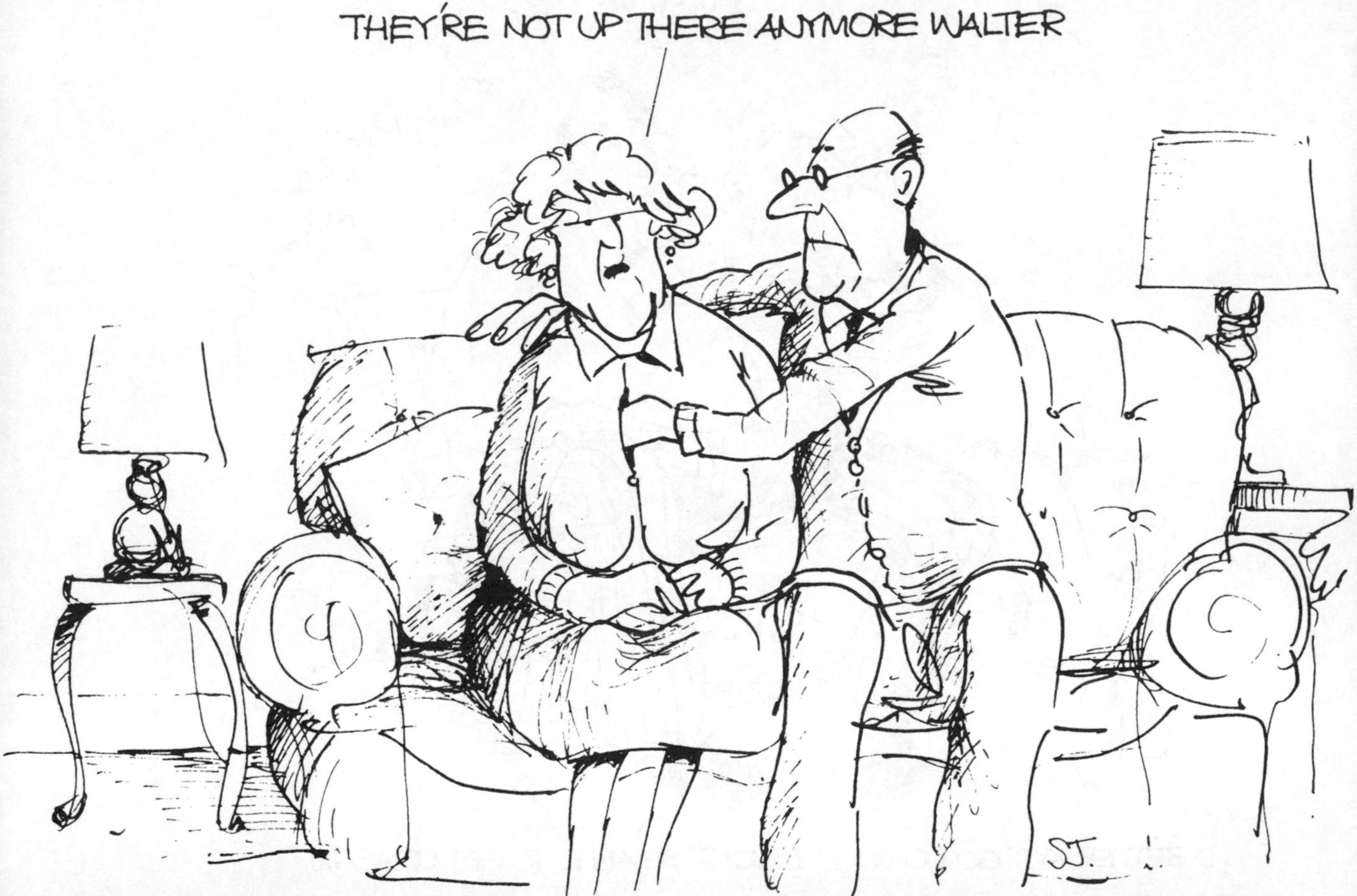
THEY'RE NOT UP THERE ANYMORE WALTER
SJ.

YOUR PERFUME IS DRIVING ME CRAZY... DEEP HEAT WAS ALWAYS MY FAVOURITE

ARE YOU GIRLS INTERESTED IN A GAME OF STRIP CRIBBAGE?

I SAID...OOH..AHH...YES..YES..OOH DON'T STOP...YES...YES..

PHEW! THESE RUBBER SHEETS GENERATE SOME HEAT DON'T THEY?

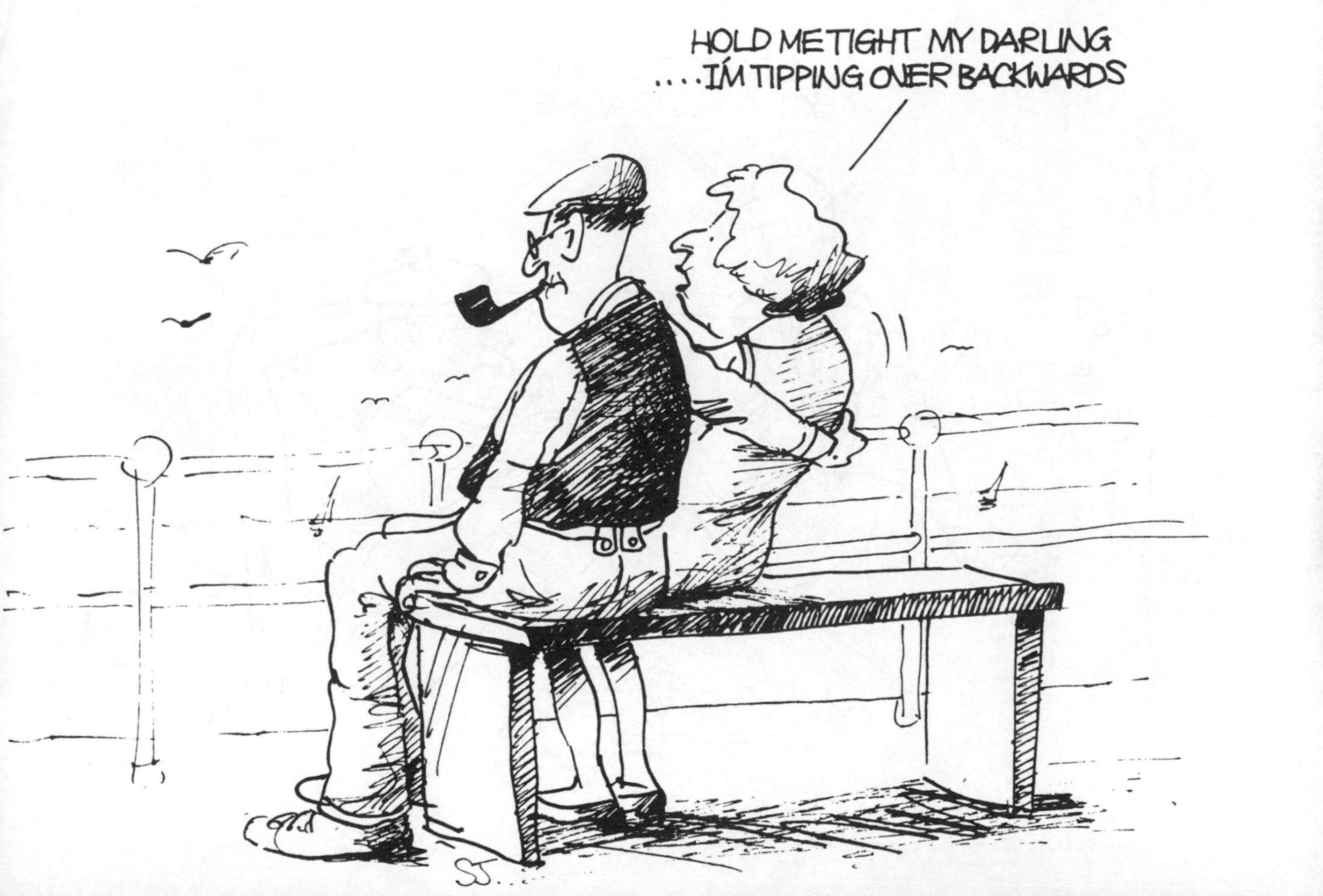
HOLD ME TIGHT MY DARLING
....I'M TIPPING OVER BACKWARDS
SJ

FOR GOD'S SAKE WOMAN GET OFF ME

WHAT WOULD YOU CHARGE FOR FIVE MINUTES LAP DANCING?

LOOK EVERYBODY - IT'S GEORGE BACK FROM HIS LITTLE TRANSPLANT OPERATION

WHAT DO YOU SAY WE POOL OUR PENSIONS AND GET A HOTEL ROOM?

OTHER GREAT TITLES FROM LITTLE **BLACK**DOG LIMITED

The fine cultivated shops carrying our titles really do get ticked off if you buy direct from the publisher so, if you can, please patronise your local gift and card shop and let them make a bob or two. If however, the fools don't carry a particular title, you can order them from us. Credit cards accepted for orders of three or more items.

LITTLE PAPERBACKS: RRP £2.99 to £3.50

FUN MINTS: RRP £1.99

SENIOR MOMENTS SIGNS: RRP £4.99

Distributed by LITTLE **BLACK**DOG LIMITED
Unit 3 Everdon Park
Heartlands Business Park
Daventry
NN11 8YJ

Tel:	01327 871 777
Fax:	01327 879 222
E Mail:	info@littleblackdogltd.co.uk
Web:	www.littleblackdogltd.co.uk

You can order other Little books directly from Little Black Dog. All at relevant retail prices each including postage (UK only)
Postage and packing outside the UK: Europe: add 20% of retail price Rest of the world: add 30% of retail price